CHAPTER ONE

I am nobody to write on a great topic like kundalini energy. I am a student of meditation working on my inner energies , so I have some understanding of inner energies that I want to express in this book.

What is this primordial force which has fascinated our existence. How to touch that greater energies within us. In spiritual world it is very central concept.

Entire civilization of humanity is involved in matter. Mind is jumbling of thought only. Beyond the domain of thoughts there is inner energies within us. This inner primordial energy is the greatest potential within us. What is the origin of this great mystic potential energy within us.

Actually during the birth of the child at the time of formation of embryo this primordial energy helps in formation of embryo. After

the formation of child this primordial energy sits and stabilised itself in the base of our spine. It is very difficult for a child to hold this higher vibrational states. So this primordial energy sits in the base of our spine in a very dormant manner.
Through certain meditative technique this energy can be ascended to higher form. Entire religion and mysticism is involved in ascending this spiritual energy. Now the question that arises from here

is that what is the nature of this great energy.
To understand this we have to understand our evolution as a human being. We are not a isolated individual. We have our origin from this primordial nature. Forces and energy that are involved in evolution of this universe are also involved in evolution of human body. Cosmic and primordial force of nature sits dormant within us in the form of great energy known as kundalini energy. Meaning

of the word kundalini is coiled. This higher force resides within us in coiled format at the base of our spine. Through certain spiritual and meditative technique this primordial force can be evoked and ascended to higher form. This higher spiritual energy is the basis of our existence. Now the important question that arises from here is that how to touch that great primitive primordial energy. To do this we have to touch some of the basic fountains of our existence. This basic fountain is breath , mind, hunger and sexuality. Each of these fountains have created a entire spiritual science of its own. For example science of breath and its pattern has created a entire science of pranayama. Central prana within us is a part of para shakti in this universe. When through certain breathing techniques we expand this central prana operating within us then we are able to evolve para shakti or kundalini energy within us. Breath has got a great interelation with our mind. Any change in pattern of our breath always create a change in pattern of our mind. To appreciate this you have to observe your breath and mind in various fluctuations of your moods. When we are in deep sorrow then the pattern of breath become very shallow in us. In deep meditation pattern of breath become very deep. If you are

a sincere and honest student of spirituality then you can easily observe the magic of breath within you.
When you are in sorrow try to focus your mind on your breath. Concentrate more and more on your breathing pattern.When you will concentrate more on your breathing pattern then you will find that your breath will become more subtle and state of your mind changes to a more joyful one.Concentrating your mind

on your breath will definately create a change in your pool of consciousness.

CHAPTER TWO
UNDERSTANDING SOUND AND MANTRAS

Purpose of this book is to understand kundalini shakti. Concept of mind , sounds , vibrations and mantra are very much central to understand this. Our mind is full of thoughts .Thoughts are actually subtle sounds in the vibrational nature of consciousness. When we speak something then that sound has external vibration and meaning. When we are thinking something then that is internal vibration only.Thinking is more subtle thought.Thoughts ultimately creates a component of feeling within us.Now there are sound waves which don't have any meaning , they are pure sound like a sound of flute.

Mantras are actually sound waves that creates a impact on our inner consciousness. In ancient text they are called as seed mantra which can create a certain change in the centre of consciousness within us.

These seed mantras are when given a proper environment then can create a tremendous change in our inner consciousness .They are provoke the primordial fire within us that is known as kundalini fire. When this fire is evoked then it can absorb all the suffering within us. Sounds are always basic to our existence. Every form of thought has got a form attached with it. Thought and form are always very much interlinked with each other. In our world of communication language and words has got a meaning attached with it. But mantras are sound waves which are vibrations that create a impact on our consciousness. For example omkar is a sound wave which signifies the state of consciousness within us.

First of all we have to understand the power that we want to evoke within us.Cosmic consciousness is hidden within our spine in the form of a hidden energy. This energy can be evoked through various mechanism. One of the mechanism is through mantras which are powerful sound vibrations. This vibration can evoke the primordial primitive force within us.

The pathway of kundalini shakti is inside in our inner world. This primordial force is the most essential part of our existence. Human existence is always in the search of completeness. This deficiency and search of completeness within us is very much eternal. Externally we are always trying to procure more and more things and internally our energy levels are always deficient. We have to look inwards to satisfy that deficiency occuring within us.

CHAPTER THREE

EFFECT OF BREATH ON OUR INNER ENERGY LEVELS

Students of mysticism have done a great study to understand the effect of breath on our inner energy levels. Breath is very much related to inner energy levels within us. Pattern of breathing is closely related to states of mind and inner energy levels within us. You can do a simple experiment on yourself. When you feel low in your life concentrate on your breath and take a deep breath and focus your mind on that breath. You will always find that on concentrating on deep breath state of your mind changes. We are able to come out of the grooves of our mind with the help of concentration on our breath. A entire science of breath is developed in this context. Any school of mysticism in this world has got a close association on our pattern of breathing. This pattern of breathing is closely associated on our inner thoughts and perception. A small spark of kundalini shakti can be provoked with the help of breathin pattern within us. This holy fire lies deep inside our spine . On provoking this fire life takes a different dimension both inside and outside us.This expanded energy is one of the finest force operating within us. Sadhakas all over the world are doing great deal of mystic practices to provoke that great force within us. Our inner world is such a great and magnificient entity that it has surprised humanity from eternity. Deep within us there is a great force of spiritual ecstasy within us. This spiritual force is great power of god within us. What is god actually? God is the great force within us that has got the potential to satisfy all the deficiency within us. Our mind is always craving to get something in our life both externally and internally.This craving is satisfied when we go deep inside and touch that great kundalini force within us. What is the nature of this force.As far as my understanding goes this force is as vast as this entire universe.This force is as magnificent as this entire universe.Only we have to look inwards to find that great force within us.I am nobody to discuss that great force. All the ego and images within should be melted to find that ultimate reality known as god. This force is very much close to life and it touches all the basic fountains of life. Touching the thread of breath can provoke this primitive energy. Fasting and concentrating our mind inwards also helps , because hunger is the most basic fountain of life. Inside us there is great fountain of consciousness which can transcend any form of reality in this world.

To understand kundalini shakti we should understand the nature of our mind. Mind has got immense energy within us. This energy is the greatest force of consciousness operating within us. Don't understand this mind as the form of brain. Brain and neuron are just a medium of travel of great energy within us. This energy operates and make us work. It take us to a great domain of dreams where we are able to create a entire world of virtual reality within us. Again this force took us to a state of deep sleep which energies our entire domain of internal energies. Again after waking up we operate again with that great energy. If you want to understand the power of this great domain then we should know the power of sleep. If we are not able to get proper sleep for few days then it become quite difficult for us to operate in the waking reality.

Now the question that arises from here is that is there any other state of consciousness other than waking, dreaming and sleeping. This is the domain of exploration that kundalini shakti wants. What happens when consciousness expands to a higher dimension. According to the great dimension of mystic literature there are dimensions and domains beyond the world of waking, dreaming and deep sleep. There are world of consciousness beyond also .This world can be understood through breath , mind , fasting and meditation. This great dormant energy within us is sitting in the deep recess of spine within us. Sexuality is the only medium of experiencing that great domain of consciousness that too in a descending form. Joy that we experience in sexuality is just the one percent of the great joy of kundalini energy within us.See what may be the great valour of that great force operating within us.Touch that reality and believe me that your life will be transformed forever. Great yogis and mystics have touch that reality and found out that great force of kunadalini shakti operating within us.Great saint of maharashtra gyaneshwar maharaj have quoted in his great book gyaneshwari that on touching the thread of breath we can go to any great dimension of consciousness within us. According to ancient mystic text our energy centers has got six layers of existence. The basic layer and foundation of our existence is muladhar which is the center of thoughts, sexuality and gross materialistic desire. This centre is present at the base of our spine. The beej mantra for this center is lam and it lies at the base of our spine. Centre above is swadhisthan which is center associated with energies of moon. This is the center attached with the force of imagination and visualization within us. Concentrating on this center increase the power of visualization within us. This center is between umbilicus and base of spine .The seed mantra for this center is vam. Center at the level of umbilicus is the manipur chakra.THis center is the center of passion and higher energies within us.This is the force of passion within us.Seed mantra for this centre is ram. Then comes the great centre of anhata at the level of heart . This is the center of compassion and feeling within us. Seed mantra for this center is yam. Then comes the center of purification within us. This is neck center at the level of neck. Seed mantra for this center is ham. This center purifies everything within us. Then we can concentrate on great center of intution within us which lies between two eyebrows. This is agnya chakra.Seed mantra for this center is om .Then we can concentrate on the top of our forehead.

This is the center of higher expanded state of consciousness.On touching this center dimensions of our living changes.This is the epicenter of our consciousness.

CHAPTER FOUR
MIND , MATTER AND KUNDALINI ENERGY

According to you what is kundalini energy.Is it only the mystic psychic force or it is something else.What is the association of kundalini and mystic energy with the huge material world of existence. To understand this we have to understand the nature of matter operating within us.This entire material world of existence is nothing but a state of vibrations.Matter and wave are interrelated with each other . Actually matter is condensed for of psychic vibrations operating within us.When we meditate more and more then there is arousal of kundalini force within us.This kundalini

force creates a control over entire material world of existence.
Then what is mind?
Mind is that inner medium within us which carries all the mystic potentials and power of kundalini force.LIfe can not be better that the feel of mystic and higher expanded field of consciousness within is. It the end result of our all the searches.It is ultimacy of all the journey that we are taking always.Actually mind ,

matter and kundalini energy is very much closely interrelated with each other.On touching this great force life become a great experience for us.That's why all the mystic of this world are trying to touch that higher force within us.This force can do anything in this world.It is the reply of all the search that human being are going through.

Nothing can be more fascinating in this world than understanding death and life. What happens after death ?

A big question mark.

Lot of belief and disbelief? Spiritual books say something that you have to blindly believe because belief is the evidence of things unseen .Science has got a limited exploration on this field. There are some people who wants to leave this domain and wants to enjoy life till death comes. There is also lot of fear , agony and tragedy related to death . It is ultimately end of everything.

My entire book is on understanding death and life after death. All of my reasoning that I will use in this book is based upon my personal experiences in deep meditation . Readers are fully free to believe and disbelieve but it is my guarantee that this book will be a great food of thoughts for them and if they try to meditate then they will realize the same reality operating within them.

My individual approach toward understanding death has always been very much scientific and analytical .

But dear science is that set of experimentation and belief that is part of collective consciousness of our civilization. There can be your individual truth and science also . An individual reality is throbbing within you. Only you have to go for a keen observation within yourself .

Soul of the reasoning used in this book is based on mysticism , religion and occultism which is understood by deep practices of meditation and self observation.

One of the major purpose that I want to fulfill from this book is to make my readers a great student of self observation , that is observation of there own mind. Mind wants to understand mind . It is the only thing in this world which has got the potential to understand it's own nature. Irony of life is that we know so much about so many things but we know nothing about us.

CHAPTER ONE
DEATH: END OF BODY AND MIND

Death is the end of the physical body, everyone in this world will easily agree on that. But what about mind ?

Many people have doubt on that whether death can end your mind .

To understand this topic we have to understand mind first. What are the component of mind that we have.

One very evident thing about us is our conscious mind , that component of mind which takes data from external world through our senses and reciprocates through thoughts and words.This kind of mind operates in our waking state of consciousness.

Another part of our mind is subconscious mind , which doesn't take data from external world of senses but it creates it's own images , thoughts and visualizations. You can relate subconscious mind in your dreaming state of consciousness. In dreaming state all of your sensory organs like eye , ears and nose are closed but you are able to create your individual reality inside yourself . This dreaming state is correct depiction of your subconscious mind. Subconscious mind is as real as waking state but without the help of external sensory organs . But there is a concrete difference between waking and dreaming state . In waking state we woke up in the same reality daily but in dreams reality changes daily.

There is another state of consciousness known as deep sleep in which all the impression of mind goes off and we move into a zone of reality in which there is no impression of mind and we move into a state of consciousness which re- energize our body and mind . Now the question that arises from here is that is there any other state of consciousness other than waking , dreaming and deep sleep.

Answer to this question is yes. There is another state of consciousness other than waking , dreaming and deep sleep known as turiya which can be explored in deep state of meditation . There is many other state of consciousness other than turiya also.

Now I am returning to my original topic that is , what is death .

Death is actually end of physical body and conscious mind .

Subconscious mind and our deeper energy states continues there journey after death also.

So dear readers , Mystery is solved. Answer is big no . From here mystery of life and death starts.

Question that arises from here is that if subconscious mind and deeper energy states are immortal then where they go after death and how they come back again in the form of physical body . What is the mechanism to do so.

To understand this we have to understand the journey of subconscious mind and deeper energy states.

For people who have mastered the science of

self observation, appreciating inner state of consciousness is very much easy for them. Problem with our modern education system is that we are never tought how to look inside us. Inner world is always filled with jumbling of thoughts, images and visualizations.

We don't know how to go beyond that.

Only deep meditation can help us to appreciate the state of consciousness operating within us.

CHAPTER TWO

JOURNEY OF SUBCONSCIOUS MIND

So in first chapter I have explained that death is the end of physical body and conscious mind. Subconscious mind and deeper energy states are immortal.

But if subconscious mind is immortal then what is the journey that it follows.

From here the mystery will take a new course . The course that you have never heard off. Since the conscious mind with the help of physical body have occupied a world known as this physical world of reality . In the same manner subconscious mind has got it's world and it's own body . This is known as astral world and astral body . Yes dear friends subconscious mind moves into a journey of astral world.

Now the most important question is that what is the astral world ?

Astral world is greater world of reality than this physical world. Infact our physical world hangs like a basket below the great astral world . In our dreaming state of consciousness we are actually residing in astral world of reality. This is the world in which energies of consciousness creates its own reality in the same manner as if reality is created in dreaming state of consciousness.

In astral world also there are various levels of existence . Lower, middle and higher . Most of the people that die in physical world go to lower astral world of reality in which they suffer there karmic channels. And when there karmic load is woven off then they return again to physical world of reality.

Only the people who have taken there state of consciousness to the state of nirbikalpa samadhi can only go to higher astral world known as hiranyaloka.

CHAPTER THREE
WHAT IS ASTRAL WORLD ?

To understand astral world we have to understand reality as a whole. What is common between humans, plants, animal and inanimate reality. If you will observe honestly then you find that among all the form of reality one thing is common and that is they all are conscious or aware to certain degree.

Every living and non living things have got certain degree of awareness. In non living matter also there are electrons and protons moving and certain degree of magnetic and electric field operating within them. Now this consciousness that operates in non living and living matter has got a certain degree of awareness which cab expand and contract in certain degrees.

So astral world is a state of consciousness or

awareness which is like dreaming state . It is as real as physical world but operates in the domain of subconscious mind .

Now what is subconscious mind ?

With every conscious actions and thoughts operating within us the impressions go to our subconscious mind. It is such a vast library which has got impressions from many lives.

All of our karmic impressions have there subtle seeds in subconscious mind which is the root cause of sufferings that we have in this world.

In a more subtle reality it is the interlink between mind

and matter. Dreams are typical depiction of the way in which mind materialize itself. Reality that we experience in dreams is as powerful than waking reality.

CHAPTER FOUR
WORLD BEYOND ASTRAL REALM

So uptil now we have tried to understand that beyond the waking state of reality there is a dimension known as astral world which is like dreaming state for us . So after our death we move to dreaming state of reality in which we experience astral reality. This astral world operates according to our karmic channels. The highest astral world is known as hiranyaloka in which advance spiritual beings who have experienced the state of nirbikalpa samadhi can go. Now the question that arises from here is that is there any other realm of existence other than dreaming reality or astral world.

Answer to this question is yes. There is another

section of our reality that is known as causal world in which our mind is in the state of deep sleep.

Who are the people who are able to reach causal world?

Beings who are in higher astral realm like hiranyaloka , when they do lots of spiritual practices then they are able to reach the dimension of causal reality. Causal world operates on undifferentiated Spiritual matter . Only very high evolved spiritual beings are able to reach causal world.

So dear friends there are many overlapping zones of reality operating in our world . They are independent and very much overlapped between each other . You can experience them in your day to day life .

Whatever you experience in waking state of consciousness is not the reality in dreaming state . Your individual reality changes in dreaming state . In deep sleep everything goes off and our mind is very much re energized.

So death is not the end . It is start of the new journey in which we have to come back again and again. So in my book I am trying to favour the science of reincarnation. Only body and conscious mind dies . Subconscious mind and inner energies have a immortal course. After death they move from physical to astral realm and come back again.

How to realize these states of consciousness operating within us?

In deeper state of consciousness we can easily realize the state of mind and consciousness expanding and contracting within us. This expanding reality can be experienced and seen in deeper state of being . In field of consciousness there are realm beyond and realm below also. We have to do lots of hard work to experience these states of consciousness.

If we have access to expanded field of

consciousness then it can do magic in our lives.

CHAPTER FIVE

LIVING A FEARLESS LIFE

What is the greatest fear that a human being can experience in his life. I think it is the fear of death . But friends when we understand states of consciousness and life beyond death then many of our fears are melted away .

What a free and beautiful life is this . We all have a

unending journey of existence. Life flows from one dimension to another dimension. There is no end to this flow of life.

Journey of subconscious mind is beyond the dimension of physical body. Even the life is not a static phenomenon . It has got the ever expanding components. In deep meditation you can experience these states of consciousness. Understanding this knowledge can make us free from great fears of life. Whatever pains we have in waking state of consciousness is temporary in nature. With the help of your mind you can go beyond these pains and sufferings. All the spiritual knowledge have been interwoven in these layers of consciousness.

Our modern education is very much physical in nature. They are not able to grant us the great knowledge of consciousness. With this knowledge our entire life can be transformed.

So look within , search within and find within to experience the higher dimensions of reality operating within you. This higher dimension of reality can pierce into any domain of our existence. You can convert yourself from a ordinary human being to a great human being . A human mind which can pierce into any domain of reality operating in this world.

This knowledge is able to give us freedom from the fear of death . One of the greatest puzzle and blockage arising in our mind . A fearless and compassionate human being is the need of this society.

Printed in Great Britain
by Amazon